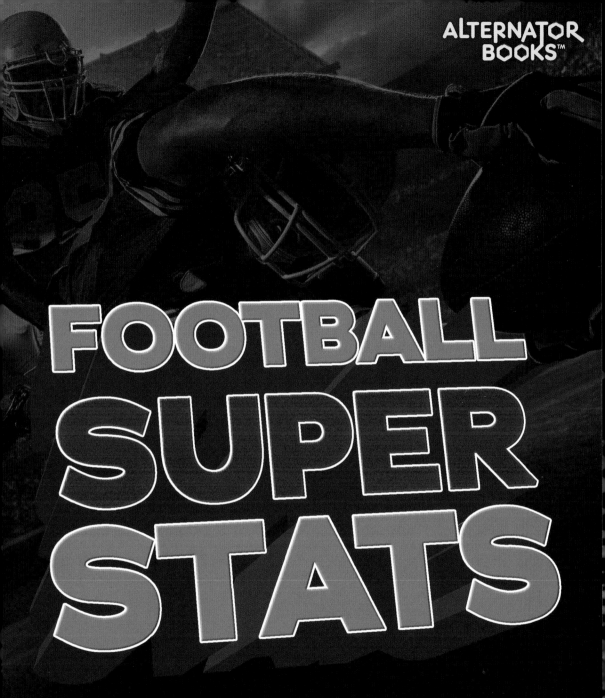

FOOTBALL SUPER STATS

JEFF SAVAGE

Lerner Publications ◆ Minneapolis

Statistics are through the 2015 National Football League season unless otherwise noted.

Lerner Publications Company
A division of Lerner Publishing Group, Inc.
241 First Avenue North
Minneapolis, MN 55401 USA

For reading levels and more information, look up this title at www.lernerbooks.com.

Main body text set in Aptifer Sans LT Pro 12/18.
Typeface provided by Linotype AG.

Library of Congress Cataloging-in-Publication Data

The Cataloging-in-Publication Data for *Football Super Stats* is on file at the Library of Congress.
ISBN 978-1-5124-3408-8 (lib. bdg.)
ISBN 978-1-5124-4946-4 (eb pdf)

Manufactured in the United States of America
1-42044-23914-1/18/2017

TABLE OF CONTENTS

POPULARITY CONTE

otball has become America's most popular sport. In 19
BC network used just two cameras to air TV's first pro
ame. The 2016 Super Bowl was covered from every ang
tched by 112 million people. Over time, fans have seen
s to the National Football League (NFL). New rules and
ent, huge indoor stadiums, and incredible TV technolog
changed the game. But one thing has stayed the same
ess of statistics (stats).

se stats to judge players and teams. Teams use stats t
s during games. For example, a team may run the ball
ainst a defense that usually allows a lot of rushing yar
are football's greatest and most important statistics? F
now a little about the sport's history.

PLATOON SYSTEM

In football's early years, most players stayed on the field all the time. They played offense, defense, and **special teams**. This was known as one-platoon football. In 1943 Sammy Baugh of the Washington Redskins led the NFL in passing accuracy on offense and **interceptions** caught on defense. He also led the league in punting yards per kick. Ernie Nevers set the record for most points scored by a player in a game. He scored six touchdowns and kicked four extra points on Thanksgiving Day in 1929. The 40-point record still stands.

One-platoon football is still used by many high school teams. But in college football and the NFL, it is a thing of the past. Each player focuses on one job in the NFL and college, and it shows in their stats.

DELPHIA EAGLES

PLAYING GAMES

Until 1946 NFL teams played between 10 and 12 games each season. From 1947 to 1960, schedules were set at 2 games. Then, from 1961 to 1977, teams played 14-game schedules. In 1978 the season expanded to 16 games, where it remains. When comparing stats, keep the era in mind—and the number of games played per season.

2016 DENVER BRONCOS

CHAPTER ONE

PLAYER SUPER STATS

PASSING FANCY

Tossing a perfect pass into the arms of a receiver for a touchdown is the dream of many athletes. A quarterback who throws a lot of touchdown passes has complete command of the field. He knows where players will be before they get there.

PEYTON MANNING

Most Career Touchdown Passes

PLAYER	TEAM*	TOUCHDOWN PASSES
Peyton Manning	Indianapolis Colts	539
Brett Favre	Green Bay Packers	508
Tom Brady	New England Patriots	428
Drew Brees	New Orleans Saints	428
Dan Marino	Miami Dolphins	420
Fran Tarkenton	Minnesota Vikings	342
John Elway	Denver Broncos	300
Eli Manning	New York Giants	294
Warren Moon	Houston Oilers	291
Johnny Unitas	Baltimore Colts	290

*The player spent most of his career with this team.

WHOOPS! WRONG JERSEY

One record Brett Favre would rather not hold is all-time most interceptions thrown. He threw more passes in his career than anyone else, so other teams had a lot of chances to intercept the ball. It's not unusual for great quarterbacks to throw a lot of interceptions. Of the top 20 leaders in interceptions thrown, 13 are in the Pro Football Hall of Fame.

BRETT FAVRE

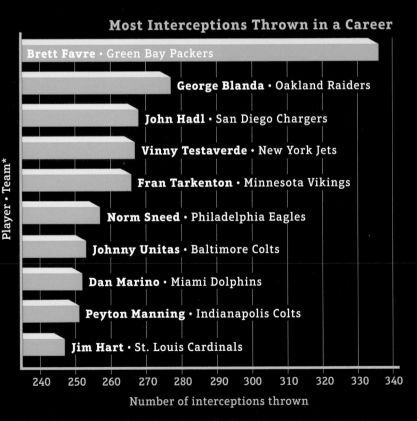

Most Interceptions Thrown in a Career

Player • Team*

- **Brett Favre** • Green Bay Packers
- **George Blanda** • Oakland Raiders
- **John Hadl** • San Diego Chargers
- **Vinny Testaverde** • New York Jets
- **Fran Tarkenton** • Minnesota Vikings
- **Norm Sneed** • Philadelphia Eagles
- **Johnny Unitas** • Baltimore Colts
- **Dan Marino** • Miami Dolphins
- **Peyton Manning** • Indianapolis Colts
- **Jim Hart** • St. Louis Cardinals

240 250 260 270 280 290 300 310 320 330 340

Number of interceptions thrown

*The player spent most of his career with this team.

T RATES

one quarterback threw 30
own passes for the season while
threw 18? Who had the better
uppose the 30-touchdown
back also threw 30 interceptions,
he 18-touchdown quarterback
ust five. Who had the better year?
erback rating measures how well
er played. In 2015 the average
uarterback rating was 90.4.

NICK FOLES

Best Quarterback Rating for a Season

YEAR	PLAYER	TEAM	RATING
2011	Aaron Rodgers	Green Bay Packers	122.5
2004	Peyton Manning	Indianapolis Colts	121.1
2013	Nick Foles	Philadelphia Eagles	119.2
2007	Tom Brady	New England Patriots	117.2
2013	Peyton Manning	Denver Broncos	115.1
2014	Tony Romo	Dallas Cowboys	113.2
1994	Steve Young	San Francisco 49ers	112.8
1989	Joe Montana	San Francisco 49ers	112.4
2014	Aaron Rodgers	Green Bay Packers	112.2
1946	Otto Graham	Cleveland Browns	112.1

RUMBLING, BUMBLING, STUMBLING

For a running back, rushing for 1,000 yards in a season is the mark of a great year. Dallas Cowboys star Emmitt Smith did it 11 straight times on his way to more career rushing yards than anyone else. In 1972 Dave Hampton became the first Atlanta Falcons player to reach the 1,000-yard mark. The game was stopped in celebration, and Hampton was given the game ball in his honor. But later in the game, he was tackled for a loss. He finished the season at 995 rushing yards. (He finally topped 1,000 yards for good in 1975.) Only six times has a team had two players achieve the feat in a season.

EMMITT SMITH

Teams with Two Players Who Gained 1,000 Rushing Yards in a Season

YEAR	TEAM	PLAYER	YARDS
2009	Carolina Panthers	Jonathan Stewart	1,133
		DeAngelo Williams	1,117
2008	New York Giants	Brandon Jacobs	1,089
		Derrick Ward	1,025
2006	Atlanta Falcons	Warrick Dunn	1,140
		Michael Vick	1,039
1985	Cleveland Browns	Kevin Mack	1,104
		Earnest Byner	1,002
1976	Pittsburgh Steelers	Franco Harris	1,128
		Rocky Bleier	1,036
1972	Miami Dolphins	Larry Csonka	1,117
		Mercury Morris	1,000

JERRY RICE

CATCHING ON FAST

As a child, Jerry Rice caught bricks while working for his father, a bricklayer. The boy liked running on the dirt road in front of his house, cutting back and forth. Rice didn't know it at the time, but he was training his body to become the greatest NFL wide receiver ever. He and Brett Favre are the only non-kickers to play in more than 300 NFL games. Rice holds nearly all the league's career receiving records.

Most Career Catches

PLAYER	TEAM*	CATCHES
Jerry Rice	San Francisco 49ers	1,549
Tony Gonzalez	Kansas City Chiefs	1,325
Marvin Harrison	Indianapolis Colts	1,102

Most Career Receiving Yards

PLAYER	TEAM*	YARDS
Jerry Rice	San Francisco 49ers	22,895
Terrell Owens	San Francisco 49ers	15,934
Randy Moss	Minnesota Vikings	15,292

Most Career Touchdown Catches

PLAYER	TEAM*	TOUCHDOWNS
Jerry Rice	San Francisco 49ers	197
Randy Moss	Minnesota Vikings	156
Terrell Owens	San Francisco 49ers	153

*The player spent most of his career with this team.

GETTING THEIR KICKS

Modern NFL field goal kickers are better than ever. In 1938–1939, kickers made less than 40 percent of their attempts. In the 1950s, the number rose to 48.2 percent. In the 1960s, it reached 56 percent. It has risen every decade since. Reasons for this include better field conditions and kickers who focus on one job all season.

Highest Career Field Goal Percentage (Minimum 100 Attempts)

PLAYER	TEAM*	PERCENTAGE (%)	YEARS
Dan Bailey	Dallas Cowboys	90.6	2011–2015
Justin Tucker	Baltimore Ravens	87.8	2012–2015
Stephen Gostkowski	New England Patriots	87.3	2006–2015
Steven Hauschka	Seattle Seahawks	86.8	2008–2015

Most Field Goals Made in a Season

YEAR	PLAYER	TEAM	FIELD GOALS
2011	David Akers	San Francisco 49ers	44
2005	Neil Rackers	Arizona Cardinals	40
2003	Jeff Wilkins	St. Louis Rams	39
1999	Olindo Mare	Miami Dolphins	39

* The player spent most of his career with this team.

GET THAT QUARTERBACK!

Deacon Jones was the leader of the Los Angeles Rams **defensive line** of the 1960s. Jones and his teammates on the line were called the Fearsome Foursome by fans. Jones was best known for tackling quarterbacks behind the **line of scrimmage**. But you won't find his name in the NFL record book. The **sack** was not an official stat until 1982. Jones unofficially recorded 26 sacks in 1967 and 24 more the next year. He had 173.5 sacks for his career. Jones even coined the term *sack*.

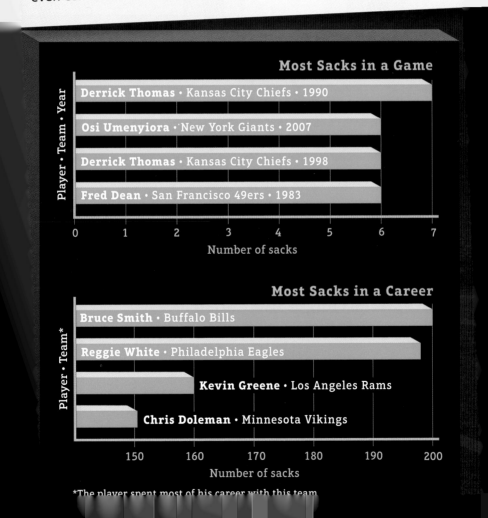

Most Sacks in a Game

Player • Team • Year

- Derrick Thomas • Kansas City Chiefs • 1990
- Osi Umenyiora • New York Giants • 2007
- Derrick Thomas • Kansas City Chiefs • 1998
- Fred Dean • San Francisco 49ers • 1983

Number of sacks: 0 1 2 3 4 5 6 7

Most Sacks in a Career

Player • Team*

- Bruce Smith • Buffalo Bills
- Reggie White • Philadelphia Eagles
- Kevin Greene • Los Angeles Rams
- Chris Doleman • Minnesota Vikings

Number of sacks: 150 160 170 180 190 200

*The player spent most of his career with this team.

I'LL TAKE THAT!

An interception can change the course of a game in an instant. A player with a knack for catching interceptions often knows where the ball will be thrown before the quarterback does. The stat measures a player's understanding of the game as well as his football skills.

RICHARD "NIGHT TRAIN" LANE

Most Interceptions Caught in a Season

YEAR	PLAYER	TEAM	INTERCEPTIONS
1952	Richard "Night Train" Lane	Los Angeles Rams	14
1980	Lester Hayes	Oakland Raiders	13
1950	Spec Sanders	New York Yanks	13
1948	Dan Sandifer	Washington Redskins	13

Most Interceptions Caught in a Career

PLAYER	TEAM*	INTERCEPTIONS
Paul Krause	Minnesota Vikings	81
Emlen Tunnell	New York Giants	79
Rod Woodson	Pittsburgh Steelers	71
Richard "Night Train" Lane	Chicago Cardinals	68

*The player spent most of his career with this team.

MVP!, MVP!

It is quite an honor to be seen as the best at what you do. Each NFL season, sportswriters vote for the player they consider to be the most valuable to his team. Peyton Manning is the only player to win the Most Valuable Player (MVP) award with more than one team. Brett Favre is the only player to win it three years in a row.

HISTORY HIGHLIGHT

Jim Brown had a shocking game at Syracuse University to end the 1956 regular season. He rushed for 197 yards, scored six touchdowns, and kicked seven extra points. It was a warning to the NFL to get ready. In nine seasons in the league, Brown led all players in rushing eight times. He never missed a game. Then he surprised everyone by retiring in 1966 and becoming an actor. He appeared in more than 30 movies, including *Mars Attacks!* and *Any Given Sunday*.

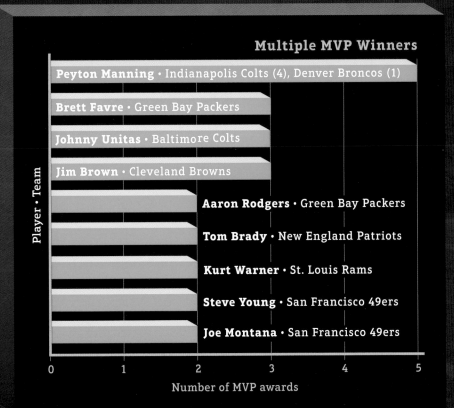

Multiple MVP Winners

Peyton Manning • Indianapolis Colts (4), Denver Broncos (1)

Brett Favre • Green Bay Packers

Johnny Unitas • Baltimore Colts

Jim Brown • Cleveland Browns

Aaron Rodgers • Green Bay Packers

Tom Brady • New England Patriots

Kurt Warner • St. Louis Rams

Steve Young • San Francisco 49ers

Joe Montana • San Francisco 49ers

Player • Team

0   1   2   3   4   5

Number of MVP awards

BRETT FAVRE

IRONMEN

Pro football is a hard-hitting sport. Players often miss games due to injury. Brett Favre had many injuries during his time in the NFL. Yet he started every game at quarterback for 19 straight seasons. Favre was finally forced to sit out a game with a serious shoulder injury that ended his career. He retired with all-time NFL records for most passes completed, most passing yards, and most passing touchdowns.

Most Games Started in a Row

PLAYER	TEAM*	TOTAL GAMES
Brett Favre	Green Bay Packers	297
Jim Marshall	Minnesota Vikings	270
Mick Tingelhoff	Minnesota Vikings	240
Bruce Matthews	Tennessee Titans	229
Will Shields	Kansas City Chiefs	223
Alan Page	Minnesota Vikings	215
Ronde Barber	Tampa Bay Buccaneers	215
London Fletcher	Washington Redskins	215

*The player spent most of his career with this team.

TOUCHDOWN!

Driving the ball into the **end zone**—that's the ultimate goal of football. Almost 120 players in NFL history have scored four touchdowns in a game. And 11 players have scored five. Chicago Bears running back Gale Sayers stands alone with six. It happened in 1965 against the San Francisco 49ers. Sayers touched the ball only 11 times on offense. He took a pass 80 yards for a touchdown. He scored four more times on running plays. His 85-yard punt return capped his record-breaking day.

STATS FACT

On November 4, 2007, Minnesota Vikings running back Adrian Peterson set the all-time record for most rushing yards in a game with 296. It was just his eighth NFL game.

Most Touchdowns in a Season

YEAR	PLAYER	TEAM	TD
2006	LaDainian Tomlinson	San Diego Chargers	31
2005	Shaun Alexander	Seattle Seahawks	28
2003	Priest Holmes	Kansas City Chiefs	27
2000	Marshall Faulk	St. Louis Rams	26

Most Touchdowns in a Career

PLAYER	TEAM*	TD
Jerry Rice	San Francisco 49ers	208
Emmitt Smith	Dallas Cowboys	175
LaDainian Tomlinson	San Diego Chargers	162
Randy Moss	Minnesota Vikings	157

*The player spent most of his career with this team.

LADAINIAN TOMLINSON

EAM SUPER STATS

NING!

o some NFL teams have winning seasons year after year? They
pported by a winning **franchise**. The owners, ticket sellers,
es, and others who make up a franchise allow the team to focus
otball. Then it's up to the players to do their part.

New York Giants joined the NFL in 1925. Since then they've
d 1,321 games, winning 697 of them. The Baltimore Ravens
n in 1996 and have won 188 games in 343 chances. How do
compare the two teams? Check out their all-time winning
entages. If a team wins half its games, the winning percentage is
The stat is a quick way to get a picture of a team's success.

Best Franchise Winning Percentages

TEAM	RECORD	WINNING PERCENTAGE
Green Bay Packers	752–568–37	.568
Dallas Cowboys	514–390–6	.568
Chicago Bears	758–573–42	.567
Miami Dolphins	449–355–4	.558
New England Patriots	491–400–9	.551
Baltimore Ravens	188–154–1	.550
Denver Broncos	478–404–10	.541
New York Giants	697–591–33	.540
Minnesota Vikings	468–407–10	.534
Indianapolis Colts	516–456–7	.531

ALMOST PERFECT

Since 1978, when the NFL season expanded to 16 games, no team has finished the entire year (including the playoffs) unbeaten. Members of the 1972 Miami Dolphins celebrate each year when the last unbeaten team loses. That's because those Dolphins remain the only modern NFL team to go undefeated in the regular season and win the Super Bowl. The 2007 New England Patriots came close. They lost the Super Bowl to the New York Giants.

2007 NEW ENGLAND PATRIOTS

Best NFL Regular Season Records since 1978

YEAR	TEAM	RECORD	PLAYOFF RESULT
2007	New England Patriots	16–0	Lost the Super Bowl
2004	Pittsburgh Steelers	15–1	Lost the Conference Championship Game
1998	Minnesota Vikings	15–1	Lost the Conference Championship Game
1985	Chicago Bears	15–1	Won the Super Bowl
1984	San Francisco 49ers	15–1	Won the Super Bowl

SUPER TEAMS

Each season the Super Bowl champion claims the Vince Lombardi Trophy. Lombardi coached the Green Bay Packers to victory in the first two Super Bowls. And 19 franchises have lifted the trophy, with 12 teams winning more than once. Four teams—the Cleveland Browns, Detroit Lions, Houston Texans, and Jacksonville Jaguars—have never played in a Super Bowl.

Super Bowl Victories

Team:
- Pittsburgh Steelers
- San Francisco 49ers
- Dallas Cowboys
- New England Patriots
- New York Giants
- Green Bay Packers
- Oakland Raiders
- Washington Redskins
- Denver Broncos
- Indianapolis Colts
- Miami Dolphins
- Baltimore Ravens

Number of titles*
(0, 1, 2, 3, 4, 5, 6)

*Includes titles won while representing other cities

BEST COMEBACKS IN NFL PLAYOFF HISTORY

Your favorite team is trailing in a playoff game by three touchdowns. Don't give up hope! Plenty of teams have rallied from behind to win in the playoffs.

1957 The Detroit Lions trailed the San Francisco 49ers by 20 points in the third quarter. The Lions were on the road and didn't have their starting quarterback. But backup Tobin Rote led his team to 24 straight points to win.

1972 The 49ers led the Dallas Cowboys by 18 points in San Francisco. But the Cowboys drew closer. Then quarterback Roger Staubach led two touchdown drives in the final two minutes to win, 30–28.

1986 The Miami Dolphins trailed the Cleveland Browns at home by 18 points. But Dan Marino passed for a touchdown and Ron Davenport ran for two more to give the Dolphins the victory.

1993 The Houston Oilers built a 32-point third-quarter lead at Buffalo. Backup quarterback Frank Reich led the Bills to five straight touchdowns. They won with a field goal in overtime. It was the biggest comeback in NFL history.

2003 The New York Giants led by 24 points at San Francisco. Then they allowed the 49ers to score the game's final 25 points. San Francisco won by one point.

2014 The Indianapolis Colts trailed the Kansas City Chiefs by 28 points in the third quarter. That's when Colts quarterback Andrew Luck took over. Luck threw three touchdowns and recovered a fumble for another. The Colts pulled off the win, 45–44.

1957 DETROIT LIONS
(IN DARK JERSEYS)

TO SCORE OR NOT TO SCORE

It's exciting to watch an explosion of offensive fireworks. Fans love scoring. But good defense wins championships. Since 1990 none of the top seven highest-scoring teams in the NFL have won the Super Bowl. But of the top seven teams that gave up the fewest points since 1990, two won the title.

2000 BALTIMORE RAVENS
(IN PURPLE)

Most Team Points Scored in a Season since 1990

YEAR	TEAM	POINTS
2013	Denver Broncos	606
2007	New England Patriots	589
2011	Green Bay Packers	560
2012	New England Patriots	557
1998	Minnesota Vikings	556
2011	New Orleans Saints	547
2000	St. Louis Rams	540

Fewest Team Points Allowed in a Season since 1990

YEAR	TEAM	POINTS
2000	Baltimore Ravens*	165
2000	Tennessee Titans	191
2002	Tampa Bay Buccaneers*	196
2006	Baltimore Ravens	201
1992	New Orleans Saints	202
2005	Chicago Bears	202
2001	Chicago Bears	203

*Super Bowl champions

THE BEST OF THE BEST

The Pro Football Hall of Fame is in Canton, Ohio. The NFL began in 1920 in Canton. When the Hall of Fame opened in 1963, 17 people were **enshrined**. As of 2016, 303 people have been voted in. Most are players. Other people close to the game, such as coaches and owners, are also enshrined. The Houston Texans and the Jacksonville Jaguars are the only two current teams not represented in the Hall of Fame by a player.

STATS FACT
Don Shula retired as coach of the Miami Dolphins in 1995. His 328 regular-season wins are the most ever. Shula coached for 33 years and had only two losing seasons.

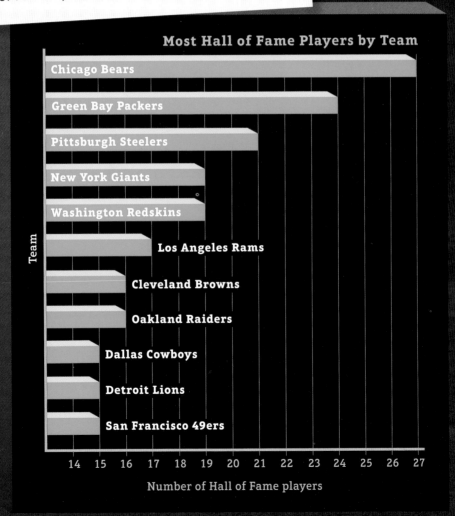

Most Hall of Fame Players by Team

Chicago Bears
Green Bay Packers
Pittsburgh Steelers
New York Giants
Washington Redskins
Los Angeles Rams
Cleveland Browns
Oakland Raiders
Dallas Cowboys
Detroit Lions
San Francisco 49ers

Team

14 15 16 17 18 19 20 21 22 23 24 25 26 27
Number of Hall of Fame players

CHAPTER THREE

STATS ARE HERE TO STAY

THE BOX SCORE

Pro football was born in 1892 in western Pennsylvania when William "Pudge" Heffelfinger was paid $500 to play in a game. Heffelfinger scored the only touchdown to win the game. Football's rules and plays have changed in many ways since. (Touchdowns counted for four points in 1892, so Heffelfinger's team won, 4–0.) One constant has been the way fans can read stats to get an idea of the action.

If you look at a box score, you can relive the action of a game from any era. Use the keys to figure out the box score on the next page.

WILLIAM "PUDGE" HEFFELFINGER

Passing Key

ATT = passing attempts
COMP = passing completions
INT = interceptions thrown

QBR = quarterback rating
TD = passing touchdowns
YDS = passing yards

Rushing Key

ATT = rush attempts
LNG = longest rush

TD = rushing touchdowns
YDS = rush yards

Receiving Key

LNG = longest catch
REC = receptions (catches)
TD = receiving touchdowns

TGT = targets (times thrown to)
YDS = receiving yards

Carolina Panthers Passing

PLAYER	COMP	ATT	YDS	TD	INT	QBR
Newton	18	41	265	1	1	55.4

Carolina Panthers Rushing

PLAYER	ATT	YDS	LNG	TD
Newton	6	45	14	0
Stewart	12	29	12	1
Whitaker	4	26	15	0

Carolina Panthers Receiving

PLAYER	TGT	REC	YDS	LNG	TD
Brown	7	4	80	42	1
Ginn Jr.	10	4	74	45	0
Olsen	9	4	41	19	0
Funchess	5	3	40	24	0
Cotchery	5	3	17	11	0

STATISTICAL EVALUATION

Fans use stats to compare players and teams. Coaches look at stats to help design game plans. **Agents** get more money from teams by using stats as evidence of players' skills. But nowhere in football are statistics studied more closely than in judging talent.

The NFL Scouting Combine is an annual event where college players spend several days doing drills and tests. Drills include running a 40-yard dash and bench-pressing 225 pounds as many times as possible. Athletes are tested on everything from how high they can jump to how quickly they can think. Coaches and scouts study their stats to help choose the players they want to **draft**.

XAVIEN HOWARD
(AT THE 2016 NFL SCOUTING COMBINE)

FANTASY AND THE FUTURE

Fantasy football is a popular game that adult fans play using the stats of NFL players. To play in a fantasy league, fans choose players to form their own teams. Teams are awarded points based on the performances of the players.

Fans usually pay an entry fee to join a league, and winners receive prizes. Many leagues last all season, and fans follow their teams on phones and other Internet devices. One study showed that 56.8 million people in the United States and Canada played fantasy sports in 2015. And 73 percent of them played fantasy football. That's a lot of fans having fun with statistics!

The NFL collects stats in new ways each season. Devices in pads, helmets, and footballs keep track of stats. We can see how fast a ball is thrown or how much force goes into a tackle. Football teams and fans want as much information as they can get, so the use of stats is likely to grow.

PLAYING FANTASY FOOTBALL

Tom Brady and Cam Newton are two of the NFL's best quarterbacks. Brady wins with great throws—and lots of them. His Patriots rank near the top of the NFL each year in pass attempts. Newton throws well, and he is a powerful runner too.

TOM BRADY

Tom Brady New England Patriots	
402	Pass completions
624	Pass attempts
64.4	Pass completion percentage
4,770	Passing yards
36	Passing touchdowns
7	Interceptions thrown
102.2	Quarterback rating
53	Yards rushing
3	Rushing touchdowns

Here are their stats for the 2015 regular season. Who is the more valuable quarterback? You decide.

Cam Newton
Carolina Panthers

Pass completions	296
Pass attempts	495
Pass completion percentage	59.8
Passing yards	3,837
Passing touchdowns	35
Interceptions thrown	10
Quarterback rating	99.4
Yards rushing	636
Rushing touchdowns	10

CAM NEWTON

agents: people who represent players. Agents negotiate contracts and other business deals.

defensive line: the players who form the front line of a defense. The defensive line's main job is to tackle ball carriers and try to sack the quarterback.

draft: choose players from a preselected pool. The NFL draft is an annual event in which teams take turns selecting players.

end zone: the area at both ends of the playing field between the goal line and the end line where touchdowns are scored

enshrined: put something in a special place to honor and preserve it

franchise: a team and the organization around it, including the owner, general manager, ticket sellers, and others

interceptions: catching passes by the defense. Interceptions result in the intercepting team taking control of the ball.

line of scrimmage: an imaginary line that runs the width of the field. The line of scrimmage cannot be crossed by either team until the ball is snapped.

quarterback rating: a statistic that describes how well a quarterback played. The number is based on catches per throw, yards gained per throw, touchdown passes per throw, and interceptions per throw.

sack: a defensive play in which one or more players tackle the quarterback behind the line of scrimmage

special teams: the group of players on the field during kickoffs, punts, field goals, and points after touchdown

Braun, Eric. *Super Football Infographics*. Minneapolis: Lerner Publications, 2015.

———. *Tom Brady*. Minneapolis: Lerner Publications, 2017.

ESPN—NFL Statistics
http://www.espn.com/nfl/statistics

Jacobs, Greg. *The Everything Kids' Football Book: The All-Time Greats, Legendary Teams, and Today's Favorite Players—with Tips on Playing Like a Pro*. Avon, MA: Adams Media, 2014.

National Football League
http://www.nfl.com

Pro Football Reference
http://www.pro-football-reference.com

PHOTO ACKNOWLEDGMENTS

The images in this book are used with the permission of: © iStockphoto.com/efks (stadium background); © Laura Westlund/Independent Picture Service, graphs and tables; © iStockphoto.com/33ft, p. 4; AP Photo/Pro Football Hall of Fame, pp. 5 (top), 24; AP Photo/Aaron m. Sprecher, p. 5 (bottom); AP Photo/Al Messerschmidt, p. 6; AP Photo/Tom DiPace, p. 7; AP Photo/Tony Gutierrez, p. 8; AP Photo/David Durochik, p. 9; AP Photo/Tony Tomsic, p. 10; AP Photo/Michael Ainsworth, p. 11; © Bettmann Archive/Getty Images, p. 14; AP Photo/Morry Gash, p. 16; AP Photo/Paul Spinelli, p. 17; AP Photo/Charles Krupa, p. 19; AP Photo/Pablo Martinez Monsivais, p. 20; AP Photo, p. 21; AP Photo/Ricky Carioti, p. 22; AP Photo/Darron Cummings, p. 26; © Mint Images/Alamy, p. 27; AP Photo/Damian Stohmeyer, p. 28; AP Photo/Al Messerschmidt, p. 29.

Cover: © iStockphoto.com/peepo (football players), © iStockphoto.com/efks (stadium).